Thank You For Your Purchase

"If everything were as it seems, there would be no need for research."

Thank you for investing in this book. Without trying to sound arrogant or anything, I want to assure you that when you complete reading this book and apply (even just a couple of) the methods taught in this book, you will be able to take your small business to the next level.

This book is dedicated to all the small business owners of the world that have taken their passion and started a business, or are planning to do so. The basic premise of the book is to share with passionate owners that to be successful in business, *passion* is good. But, *passion* is not enough!

Marketing is what allows us to profit from our passions.

Unfortunately, most small business owners just don't know what we don't know that we don't know about marketing.

Sure, we can speak the *"business speak"* when 'necessary.' And, yes, we continue to "throw" money at advertising that we aren't able to see results. And, most of us have heard of 'marketing.' But, the *"proof is in the pudding."* Small businesses are struggling. Well, at least, some are. Those that aren't are using the formulas and the systems introduced in this book.

The contents of this book are excerpted from the training program, "Small Business Marketing TOUGH LOVE SYSTEM: The Ultimate Business Growth Training System For Small Business Owners." The training program includes videos, audios, workbooks, checklists and other resources to ensure that small business owners "know" marketing, "know" how marketing works, and "know" what to do, specifically, to grow their business.

After reading this book, you will understand and "know" marketing (in today's changing business environment). And, more specifically, you will understand your business better in terms of how your customers see you and what you must do to ensure that they continue to buy from you and also be raving fans that tell their families, networks, friends and all of the world about you and your business.

If you want to ensure that you can get a measurable return on investment ROI of your advertising dollar, you should consider investing in the training program, "Small Business Marketing TOUGH LOVE SYSTEM: The Ultimate Business Growth Training System For Small Business Owners." Find out more at the back of this book.

Mindset Introduction

In some regards, business is still business. But, in many, many ways, something important has changed the way of doing business successfully.

Fortunately, the larger successful companies have spent millions of dollars and many hours of time doing the research. Their resultant marketing strategies are implemented all around us every day. The successful customer-getting formulas will be introduced and explained in this book. The formulas are not secret; they're just not well known about or understood by small business owners.

By having possession of this book, you now have the successful formula intros in your hand. The formulas are tested and proven winners. What is not proven is your Business Mindset. As a small business owner, you know by now that we small business owners are not 'regular' people. Part of what makes us different from 'regular' people is our passion for business. Passion is good—very good! In today's business environment, however, having passion is not enough to successfully grow your business.

Proper mindset is critical to your success. Your proper mindset will tell you why your #1 Job, every day in your business, is to get more customers. Your proper mindset will also tell you why your #2 Job is to service your customers in such a way that keeps them happy and generating referrals to your business. Your proper mindset will show you the actual value of your customers.

The content is this book is designed to contribute to your proper mindset for your profitable business growth marketing strategies—to get more customers and to get current customers to purchase more often.

The "Boxes" That Bind

A little about me: My career has included 20+ years in the world of professional education. I was often accused of "thinking outside-of-the-box"—to which I plead 'guilty' (with an explanation). My experience has been—and continues to be—that real life takes place and is in full effect "outside-of-the-box!" Among professional educators and academicians, if they do not "know" how to describe an experience or categorize it using the categories of their profession (their "box"), the experience is not "real" or did not happen according to their (self-declared) experts.

Don't get me wrong—I understand it! I fully understand the need for cohorts to have a 'common language' to be able to intelligently discuss and communicate within that arena. But, to proscribe that everybody that does not "limit" themselves or speak a "limiting language" is wrong for "thinking outside-of-the-boxes."

Such impediments are what prevent many very smart business owners from being as successful and profitable as they should be and want to be. They try to 'conform' to "boxes" that aren't real and will not grow their businesses. By its nature, the world of professional education is out of touch with the world as it is happening. Remember, they were the last ones to concede that the earth was not flat after all. According to them, everyone who thought or said otherwise was "outside-of-the-box." That's the track record of professional education. Even today, they unquestionably teach that the sun rises in the east.

Actually, as you probably know, the sun doesn't move east or west—the earth rotates, but, if you were in school, you must speak the language of their "box." As a smart business owner, don't let the "boxes" fool you or bind your creativity.

A successful and profitable business's growth strategy requires a clearer, honest and more accurate language (and checks and balance system) to keep their finger on the pulse of their customers' needs & desires and the formulas and systems that work effectively for them.

Your profitable business growth will not come from the language and terminology that you use (within your industry or educational background). It will start with you having the proper mindset and being clear about what is involved. The education profession has not caught up with what you will learn about growing your business in this book. So, don't look for the standard "boxes." (This isn't an indictment of the professional education industry, at all. Their heart is in the right place, but their "sense of reality" is about two years behind actual real life.)

Set your mind free!

The "New" Math – How to Value Your Customer

With the proper mindset, you will be able to see things from a very different perspective and the changed view will help your business to grow. For example, you must have the proper mindset to calculate and appreciate the lifetime value LTV of your customers. Far too many small business owners make the costly mistake of spending their marketing efforts on getting a customer for "today." When you know and truly understand the real lifetime value of your customer, you will set up sales systems to get a customer for a lifetime. Also, you will learn that spending more on getting customers for a lifetime is exceptionally profitable. Finally, you will find out that it will cost you much less of your advertising budget. Best of all, you will finally be able to track what works and does not work in your marketing strategies. To save money and make more money at the same time is a very good thing and what this book and associated training program offers.

Let's begin.

Chapter 1 - Why Customers Do & Don't Buy From You

*The **unique selling proposition** (a.k.a. **unique selling point**, or **USP**) is a <u>marketing</u> concept that was first proposed as a theory to understand a pattern among successful advertising campaigns of the early 1940s. It states that such campaigns made unique propositions to the customer and that this convinced them to switch brands. The term was developed by pioneer of <u>television advertising</u>, <u>Rosser Reeves</u> of Ted Bates & Company. <u>Theodore Levitt</u>, professor at <u>Harvard Business School</u>, suggested that "Differentiation is one of the most important strategic and tactical activities in which companies must constantly engage."[1] The term has been used to describe one's "personal brand" in the marketplace.[2] Today, the term is used in other fields or just casually to refer to any aspect of an object that differentiates it from similar objects.*

Source: Wikipedia

When teaching about the importance of knowing the unique selling proposition USP of your business, I usually start by encouraging you to ask yourself "Why should a prospect choose you over any other and every other option that's available to them, including doing nothing?"

Not having an answer to that question—or, worse yet, not having current and accurate answers from your current customers and input from your staff—means that you must go back to the basics and begin again. The more information that you have from your customers, the better you will be. When you have accurate and balanced information from your customers, you can successfully differentiate yourself from your competitors.

Here are a few methods to get the information needed:

Just Ask Your Customers: One of the easiest methods to find out what customers and potential customers want from your business is to ask them. Always ask and then act on the answers.

Survey Your Customers: Getting customers to put their opinion in writing on a survey is one of the most popular and well-established methods to obtain customer feedback.

Involve And Survey Your Staff: Your staff are the most resourceful and reliable of your customer feedback channels. Involve your staff so that they are encouraged to build strong, long-term relationships with customers so that they feel free to share how they feel about the service. It then falls upon staff to provide feedback for improving customer processes and customer service.

Use Statistics: The most significant current feedback regarding whether your customers are satisfied with your service or not is whether they continue to buy from you. Of course, while information on sales may be an accurate indicator of how well you are doing at present, it is no guarantee that you are delivering the product or service that the customer really wants.

Finding out what your customers want from your business by asking them should help you to create your unique selling propositions.

Examples of good USPs are:

> FedEx: "When it absolutely, positively has to be there next day."

<u>Remax</u>: "We'll sell your home in 90 days or we'll sell it for free."

Most USPs have some things in common:

- High competition industries and businesses
- USPs that speak to their target market
- Most target a niche within a niche
- Most are very normal, boring products or services

Let's Talk About Some Possible USP Strategies

Product/Packaging: Having a unique product package that your competitor doesn't have. A very good and successful example of this is Apple products. This USP strategy is thought to be more difficult to create because you must have the ability to legally change the product or packaging.

Personal example: As a professional photographer, I always deliver my photos in elaborate packaging. Also, I purposely have a process where customers can only have their photos delivered to them by me. My customers can see their proofs online, but I make it a special point to deliver all photos personally.

Process: You might have something unique about the way the product is constructed or about the way your customer is helped. This strategy works very well in service businesses.

Personal example: I make it a point to "over-deliver" in customer service to my photography clients. I purposely treat them like divas and I'm their personal paparazzi. They love the personal attention and don't mind paying my prices.

Personality or Persona: Putting a face on the advertising and marketing that connects with your target market. For example, you, the business owner can have your image on your marketing materials; star in your own television commercials and online videos (my favorite).

Unique or High Level of Service: Providing a unique and unbelievable service feature or level. You should come up with a way to offer a high level and unique product or service for a premium price.

Example: I already told you about my "over the top" customer service, but an even more obvious example is Starbuck's. People (including me) actually regularly stand in line to pay very high prices for their coffee beverages.

The "It" Factor That Makes ALL Good USPs Work

The "It" Factor that your USPs must have to be effective:

- Be precise enough to echo the prospect's thoughts.
- Must address the biggest objection of fear of buying.
- Must promise to solve one major problem that your potential customer will pay to have solved.
- Must include the dominant emotion driving your potential customer.

You Know Your USP Is Good When:

Customers come in and say the only reason that they came in is because of your USP and not because of your low prices.

Customers drive by your competitors' businesses, park in your competitors' parking lot because yours is too crowded, just so they can buy from you because you are their "expert…"

You MUST Give Customers A Compelling Reason To Buy From Your Business

Very Important Notes:

- No matter how great you think that your product/business/service is, if you don't have a compelling unique selling proposition USP, then you are just another faceless business in a long, very crowded list of other faceless businesses.
- No matter how good your USP is, you MUST be able to consistently deliver on your promise to your customers or you are better off not having a USP!

Chapter 2 - The Critical Significance of Your Business Brand

As business owners know, your business brand is now more important to getting customers than ever. Brand growth should be a major focus of your marketing strategies because, in today's business environment, your brand has a direct impact on your business's success and its future growth.

Although business owners have some knowledge of the value of having a business brand, many just don't know how to build a sustainable brand.

According to Hinge Marketing, your brand is made up of two criteria: your business's reputation and your business's visibility in your market. Reputation has even more impact on potential customers than your business's expertise or specialization. Businesses with the strongest brands have the best reputations. As a result, more and more buyers are very willing to refer to their friends, families and networks. Consequently, businesses with great brands get even more buying customers over time.

The best method of building a stellar business reputation is to produce great results for customers and potential customers. With a strong reputation, your business will get more customers from referrals and your marketing messages will be better remembered (customers take action based on marketing messages).

As significant as reputation is in building a strong brand, it isn't enough to achieve the best brand. Your target audience must "see you everywhere." You must be widely known to your target audience by keeping your visibility high. Your target audience must not only know that your business exists, they must also know how you can solve their problem.

Visibility is the difficult part of building a great brand for most businesses. Even those with great reputations fall short of their visibility reaching large portions of their target audiences. Business owners can remedy this problem by taking the time to research and systematize their marketing methods. They must take the time to decide exactly who they would like to reach (their perfect customer profiles), and gauge their marketing messages specifically to that audience. Look, your target market will probably only remember one thing about your business, why not make it the one thing that makes you different (and better) than your competitors?

Since visibility is the difficult part of building a great brand, let me suggest a few things that you can do to make sure that your business has 'high' visibility among your target audience:

Social Media: Use social media to dominate on platforms like Facebook, Linkedin, YouTube and Twitter. Just "being there" is not enough. You must have a clear voice online to develop your network.

Create Outstanding Content: Creating great content will allow your target audiences to see if they will know, like and trust you. Creating great content will also position you as an industry leader. Your content should be educational and informative rather than promotional.

Create Strategic Marketing Alliances: A strategic marketing alliance is a partnership in which you combine marketing efforts in order to benefit both partners. Partner with prominent institutions to take on major projects.

If you want your business to successfully get more customers and get current customers to purchase more often, branding is a must. More significantly, you more than likely need 10 brands to build a very successful and profitable business (according to business growth experts like Eben Pagan) and every one of your brands must fit and support your overall marketing strategy.

Like so many other business terms thrown around, "branding" is often misunderstood and sometimes misrepresented. Your accurate and profitable brands will be a result of your surveying your customers and creating targeted, customer-focused, marketing messaging.

Branding your business is no longer enough! You need to brand yourself. You need to brand your products. You need to brand your method of product delivery. You need to brand your methods of doing business. You need to brand the experience that you give to your customer. You must brand the differentiations that separate you from your competitors.

Just having a great product/service simply is no longer enough either! To build a profitable business by getting more customers and getting current customers to purchase more often, you need the formulas of successful businesses and the systems that grow your business for you.

Currently, successful and profitable businesses use more 'customer-focused' information and interaction to establish important business elements such as their best branding strategies and staying on top of their customers' desires and needs. In today's business environment, the businesses that best respond to the desires and needs of their customers are proving to be the most consistently profitable businesses.

To learn more and access resources click here
www.MyMarketingSystems.com

Chapter 3 - The Gift that keeps on giving – How to Get Contact Information & Build Your List

Know this: Every potential customer who walks into your business, or sees—or hears—your marketing message, is not ready to buy right then. So, you must make every effort to get the contact information of everyone who comes into contact with your business or your marketing messages. Currently, the best contact information is a collection of their email addresses. That way, you can follow up with them by sending communications, newsletters, special offers and coupons.

As a rule, people do not provide their contact information by just being asked for it. They will, however, provide the contact information in exchange for something that they perceive as "valuable." For some, it can be an invitation to join your customer loyalty program or your "special buyers" program, etc. Discount coupons also work to get customers to provide their information in exchange.

Make it a part of your sales process to request the contact information for every customer who enters your business. Determine what you will offer in exchange. Make sure that your sales staff are trained to prioritize getting all contact information. You can best do this by making it a part of your sales process and making sure that all staff members are trained how to implement your sales process.

The Power of Your List – When Used Correctly

As powerful a marketing strategy as building a list is, only 10% of American businesses keep a current list of their customers. This is in the face of statistics that show that businesses spend five times as much for new customers than they do on their current customers. Yet, a current customer is worth ten times the cost of acquiring a new customer.

To leap ahead of your competition, you must use your list to build and nurture relationships with your customers. Build relationships with customers that engender loyalty. You must gather information that is valuable to you such as age, birthdays, anniversaries, family size, etc., but, initially, just make sure that you get the basic contact information such as a physical address (for direct mail) or an email address.

Often, even the businesses that collect customer data and build a list don't know how to effectively follow up. First of all, building and nurturing a relationship is the key purpose of collecting information. Yes, you want to convert them into purchasing customers, but customers usually buy from businesses that they know, like and trust. Regularly following up with non-sales communication keeps your business top-of-mind as well as building the relationship.

Building Trust Is A Must

To build a good opt-in list you need people to trust you. For a faster and quicker build up, you need to get your opt-in subscribers to trust you quickly. The faster you build your opt-in list, the faster word-of-mouth about your site and company gets to be spread. The bigger the scope of your opt-in list, the more traffic you get, spelling more profits. It's easy math if you think about it. Getting the numbers is not that simple though— or maybe it is…

- **Getting the trust of your clientele shouldn't be so hard, especially if you do have a legitimate business**. Getting your customers trust should be based upon your expertise. People rely on other people who know what they are talking about. Garner all the knowledge and information about your business. As a rule, many businesses are started because of the passion of the owners. Share your passions.

- **Show your clients that you know what you are talking about**. Provide them with helpful hints and guidelines that pertain to what you are selling. Talk about how to install a roof if you're into hardware products or provide articles on insurance settlements if you're a settlement lawyer. If your customers see you as someone who knows what he is doing and speaking about, they will trust you quickly.

- **Be true to your customers. If you want to hype up your products and services, provide guarantees**. The more satisfied customers you get, the bigger probability there is that they will recommend you. Generally, people will trust someone they know, when that someone recommends you then you're a shoo-in. They will go to your site and check it for themselves and be given a chance to experience what the others have experienced from you, so make sure to be consistent in the service you provide.

- **Another tip in getting a customer to trust you quickly is to provide them with an escape hatch**. Show them that you are not there to trap them. Keep a clean list that would enable them to unsubscribe anytime they want. Elaborate your web form by providing information on how to unsubscribe from the list. Guarantee them that they can let go of the service whenever they want to. Many are wary that they may be stuck for life and would have to abandon their email accounts when they get pestered with spam.

Remember—when you get the trust of your clients, don't lose that trust. If you do anything with their email addresses like sell them or give them out, you will lose many members of your list as well as potential members. The true, quickest way to gain the trust of your subscribers is when you are recommended by someone they trust.

One of the best marketing strategies that you can use in your business is building a list.

An opt-in list is the best, most effective and smartest option that you can create to make it big. It is one thing to stay in business and it is another thing to have a profitable business. So, if you will be allowed to choose, make use of the building lists a priority to ensure that profits will keep coming in.

Building a list will definitely work to your benefit. This will ensure that you can maintain close contact and a good relationship with your clients, especially the frequent visitors.

This will also save you money, time and effort because once you come up with a new product or new information, you know exactly who you will send updates to because you have a definite market.

This is one aspect that you will have to maintain to have a steady source of income at the least. Then the rest of your efforts will be focused on making the number of your regular clients grow.

Some pointers in building your opt-in list:

☑ **You should put a 'subscribe link' or 'subscribe box' on your website**. It is advisable to put it on all the pages. Then make sure that it is strategically positioned, meaning it has to be easily located by the visitors. The upper right hand corner of the page would be a good position.

☑ **Promote your website and promote it even more to give it more exposure and to get more subscribers.**

☑ **Come up with contests or give away freebies** and goodies that will require visitors to give out their email addresses to be able to join.

☑ **Give out information, articles and updates to your clients** with your links included. Make sure that the information will be relevant to the client.

☑ **Offer free courses to your visitors**. This will also help maintain a good relationship with your subscribers.

☑ **Use your signature also to make your opt-in list expand**. Every time you send out messages the link information should be included.

☑ **Do some networking too**. Join some forums or discussions and build relationships with the people there. This way will also be a good way for you to get more contacts and clients.

At the same time, you should also know what you should avoid in building an opt-in list. There is one thing that you should keep in mind as the *don'ts* of building a list.

✕ **NEVER EVER spam your subscribers**. It is best that you get permission from your subscribers, or else you might end up with a bad reputation.

✕ **Avoid <u>ABRASIVE</u> pop-ups**. They can sometimes annoy your business website visitors. There are also pop-up blockers now. Your efforts here might end up futile.

✕ **You should also refrain from flooding your subscribers with information**. You might end up as an annoyance and you might not get a favorable result. There may be times that you'll give relevant information, but your clients may just dismiss it.

The benefits of having many regular subscribers are <u>undeniable</u>. They will definitely keep your business going and you will definitely enjoy the profits that will come in. Just remember that things don't end there.

Once you've built a substantial opt-in list, make sure that you maintain it well. Keep in contact with your subscribers. Send them updates. Give out special offers and helpful tips. Freebies will be helpful too.

Chapter 4 - Will They Still Love Me Tomorrow? – How to Follow Up With Customers

The harsh reality that many business owners don't want to hear is that prospects and customers always forget about your business over time. It is what it is. No matter how great your connection at the time of contact or visits to your business, the longer you wait to follow up with them, the more they forget you.

See, part of your job is to constantly present the prospect with a persuasive sales message. You want to feel as if they must come to only your business when they're ready to buy.

So, don't just sell; build a relationship by offering educational and relevant information in an entertaining way. It goes back to the educational direct mail marketing strategies that I talked about earlier.

The sad truth is that most business owners are looking at marketing as an expense instead of an investment. That's why most business owners are not trying to create a multi-step campaign that runs consistently.

But here's the secret—creating a multi-channel marketing campaign that is affordable, produces high quality leads and runs completely on auto pilot, is the secret to practically all long term successful companies. They know how to do this.

They know how to get in front of their prospect and get in front of their past customers and continue to do it in a way that's affordable and produces high quality leads.

The ugly truth is even a low quality product or service, with lousy customer service, can generate millions of dollars in sales, with a consistent follow-up marketing campaign or marketing plan.

So, even if you're doing a lot of things wrong, if you do this one thing right, you can still make a ton of profit and have a successful business.

So, why don't more business owners do it?

Here are some of the most common excuses:

- I can't afford to pay for marketing.
- I don't have my customers', or prospects' contact information.
- Even if I had their contact information, I don't know what to say.
- I don't know how to contact the customers or leads.
- I already have one million things going on at the same time.
- I don't have someone to do this for me.
- The excuses go on and on.

These are all the excuses that business owners who are failing, or floundering or struggling use.

The real danger in making so many excuses is that it quickly becomes your mindset. Your mindset has to be one that is a problem solving mindset, not one that accepts excuses and then just deals with them.

6 Methods You Can Use To Follow Up With Prospects, Leads & Customers

Follow Up Method #1: Email - The majority of North Americans have an email address; even the majority of the world has an email address that they check weekly and even daily, in most cases.

If you have a website, then you should and can send out emails. They can be scheduled weeks and months in advance. You don't have to wait until the day of your special discount offer, to send out an email. You can even use the same emails. So, once you do the initial work, you don't have to repeat it again. You can just schedule it to go out again and again on different days.

Emails can be used to send out a persuasive sales message to build your brand. An email is a great way to build relationships with your prospects and clients and, finally, it's a 100% trackable. You know who's opening it and what's working. So the first follow-up method that I would suggest for you is email. It simple and it's inexpensive. Now that you have the email address, you can use these email systems to get right in front of the prospect all the time. It's virtually free to set down.

Follow Up Method #2: Text Messaging - Text message has the highest opening rate of all communication. It's similar to when the email first came out. Everybody used to go and check their email. Now that's the same kind of open rates that you're getting with text messages. It can be used to generate instant sales and prospects and it's another effective communication tool in your marketing arsenal. Its 100% trackable, allowing you to know who's opening your messages and what's working and it only costs 1 or 2 cents per text to send out.

Follow Up Method #3: Recorded Message Voice Blasts - Most businesses don't try to make the human connection, so your message will stand out by using this method. When a customer or prospect gets a voicemail from you, they're going to be like, "Wow you took the time out to call me." They don't know you automated it and pre-recorded that message. It creates a stronger bond to your customers when they hear your voice on their answering machine or their voicemail. You can set an automated, recorded voice blast out and have a recorded campaign going in 5 or 10 minutes.

You can even create your campaign online. It's really affordable to do. Even if you have large lists of people you want to send out a message to, the cost is around about 3 - 5 cents per lead. That's a really affordable way to do a follow-up recorded message voice blast.

Follow Up Method #4: Post Cards – Postcards are still an effective way to advertise because the person who is receiving your post card is practically guaranteed to see your marketing messages.

When using postcards, your marketing message tends to be simpler and more effective because the post card is limited in size. Sometimes, when you have a whole newspaper ad, or you have a whole minute or two. When you say something, it tends to ramble a little bit, but when you get these post cards, it's going to be a simpler message, because you have a limited amount of space to get your message in.

At 43-50 cents per post card, that's still a phenomenal deal when you're making hundreds of dollars in profit from each customer.

Follow Up Method #5: Letters and Newsletters – Although many business owners are adopting newer technologies to follow up with their prospects, don't forget about the old methods like sending out letters and newsletters because those methods still work.

Your letters and newsletters can range in length from one to ten pages and allow you to tell your story in a compelling and persuasive way, generating sales. You have more space in a letter or in a newsletter than you do on a post card, so you can get more of your story out. You also can allow your customers to see behind the curtain of your business and see exactly that you're like them and desire a meaningful relationship.

This method can also be automated, therefore allowing you to create your letter once and schedule it in advance. You can do this online. It's very affordable to do and you can do this for about 50 cents per letter.

Follow Up Method #6: Live Phone Calls - This can be a customer service follow-up call or a survey to see what other products and services your customer wants from you.

Not many companies are doing these live phone calls, so you're really going to stick out with this when you make this type of connection. In this day and age, people are desperate to know that a business cares about their input and feedback. So, giving them a customer service or survey call makes them feel good and makes them feel like they're listened to, connected and very important.

It's very affordable to do because you already have phone lines in your office, so it's not like you have to set up this huge call center. Just use the phone line that you already have. It's easy enough to actually implement, because it's just a phone call.

To learn more and access resources click here
www.MyMarketingSystems.com

Chapter 5 - How to Reactivate Former Customers

Customer reactivation is when you put together a marketing campaign to present an offering to your past customers who haven't been back to your business in an unusually long period of time.

Why would you focus on past customers? Well, the fact is that the third easiest customer in the world to sell to is someone who bought from you before, but hasn't received any communication from you in months or even years.

So, why would customers NOT come back to buy from you?

- Well, number one, they're unhappy with your product or service.
- They no longer need your product or service.
- It's no longer convenient to do business with you. Meaning, they moved away, or you're no longer close to them.
- They've switched to another brand of your product or service, and they're embarrassed because they've been away too long and they don't want to disappoint you.
- Or they just plain forgot (which, by the way, is the number one reason).

But you can't blame them. It's not the customers' responsibility to remember to come back and do business with you. It's your job to remind them to come back and to do business with you.

You have to create compelling and persuasive marketing messages that communicate to your customers consistently because, when you don't stay in contact, the reality is, they don't come back.

Keep in mind that good customers are being actively pursued by other companies. Your past customers or clients may think you've gone out of business if they don't hear from you at all. Sometimes profitable customers feel like they're not valuable or appreciated and they begin to view you as a commodity provider. Then customers gradually forget about your business, because you're not staying in contact, and they begin to forget why they chose you in the first place. They start scratching their heads, asking themselves, "Why did we go there?" They never remember because you're not communicating on a consistent and regular basis.

In order for you to keep good tracking systems and know what's happening in your own business, you MUST have an electronic system in place for customer information and purchase frequency.

You've got to know answers to questions like "What's your average life cycle and life span of your average product or service?" If you simply can't remember the last time you've seen most—or all—of your last customers, it's been way too long. If they haven't scheduled for ongoing maintenance, or they routinely don't show up or reschedule, then you know it's just been too long and there's a disconnection and you're not connecting well with that customer or client.

To learn more and access resources click here
www.MyMarketingSystems.com

Chapter 6 - How to Create A Customer Reactivation Campaign

Step #1: Determine the average life cycle of your clients.

Don't get overwhelmed by this because you have dozens, or hundreds, or thousands of products. Focus on your bestselling 5 or ten products or services, then figure out the life cycle of those products, or when customers should be coming back to get services, maintenance, all those kinds of things.

Just focus on the time frame of when you usually see customers come back, and make a note of the average frequency.

For example: if, on average, you see a customer every 6 months, or every 4 or 5 weeks etc., make a note of it and you could average it out.

A car dealer may go back as far as 5 or 10 years to find out the average frequency of purchases, while a chiropractor may only need to go back every 6 months.

So you have to look at your business—and your business model and your products and services—and figure out the average life cycle to see when customers should be coming back.

Step 2: Create a mailing list of your past customers. Use the average purchase frequency to create a date range at least. Use every piece of information you have ever collected about your customers to create a list of similar customers. Focus only on the most profitable customers and don't be afraid to create several lists of similar customers.

For example: you could do something like this:

List 1- 500 customers bought product A

List 2- 300 customers brought product B

Step 3: Create your offer. Your offer to these past customers should be a really attractive offer. Stay away from the generic discounts and offers. Be sure to include a good until date on your offer. You don't want to leave an offer hanging out there forever. You want to create a sense of urgency and an end date on it.

This should be a 3 or 4 step mailing campaign. You can do this with 3 or 4 steps with a mailing campaign. Also sign them up with your loyalty program, so, once you get them, make sure you put an ad talking about your loyalty program. Use this as another opportunity to get your loyalty program in front of your past customers.

Step 4: This step is scheduling your campaign. Your marketing actions should be about 5-7 days apart. Schedule the entire marketing campaign in advance, this is so important, so you just have to set it up once, and then it's on auto pilot.

You want it to be automated, where you can press a button and it happens. Be sure to take into consideration holidays and weekends. You want it to be successful. So there is no need to be mailing it on a Sunday. Take into consideration holidays. Don't do it at the wrong time of year, because it will fall flat. Make sure you're properly staffed and have scripts prepared for your reactivation campaign.

So if you're going to do a key product, or some type of special offer, make sure your employees and your staff and your sales people know what the offer is. You should have a print out or copy of the mail pieces that you use in the office so that everyone can see exactly what customers are talking about and what they're receiving.

To learn more and access resources click here www.MyMarketingSystems.com

Chapter 7 - How to Build A Superstar Sales Team

See, the simple truth is every business has a sales team, even if they don't want to admit it. Any staff member or employee who has contact with a prospect, lead or customer can influence a buying customer.

Many business owners are in denial about their sales team. So if you have staff who don't think of themselves as sales people, they're still influencing buying decisions. That includes the secretary who answers the phone and your back office support people who are providing support. They're all sales people because they have influence over a buying decision.

So now I'm going to talk about the blueprint that you need for building your sales team.

Phase one is creating your sales presentation blueprints.

Use the research you've already done from the previous module to create your sales blueprint presentation for face to face interactions, over the phone sales, online sales imprint sales and processes for converting former customers into new customers. You want to create a training notebook or a training guide or training manual with all of your best sales scripts and materials.

You're going to tap into all of the experience that you had—the research, the knowledge, the tools that your best sales team has, or even your best employees have—and begin to compile that so that you can begin to create these sales presentations.

Your sales presentation blueprints are the road maps for yourself and your staff to follow religiously. It's what you use to train new hires, or to train existing employees who are just not hitting the mark. They must be well thought out and so simple to understand that literally a cave man could do it. You want it to be, "Do this. Say that. Go there. Do this. Give them this form." You want it to be super simple, but it should be detailed and give the reader—the employee—a detailed explanation from the initial greeting of a customer or prospect to the last thing to say to the customer (prospect) as they are leaving, with or without buying.

So once again, you want to have the exact process mapped out. These are the major questions you have to ask, the information that you are trying to gather from a prospect, the final thought that you want from a prospect if they leave without buying. All these things need to be mapped out. Don't assume anything. You would be amazed at things employees should know, but don't know.

So, in phase one, create your sales presentation blueprint by gathering all information from your successful sales presentations and then compile that information and create that training manual, and then make that your best practice.

The Core Components of Your Sales Scripts

Here are the core components of all your sales scripts, no matter what you're doing, who you're focusing on.

- Greeting
- Exploratory questions
- Product or services recommendations
- Low pressure close
- Upsell, down sell or cross sell

So, let's cover the greeting, this is where 99% of business owners make their first and biggest mistake when they're trying to convert leads into customers.

The worst type of greeting is, "How may I help you?" or "Can I help you find something?"

It's terrible. Instead of asking, "How may I help you?" start with something like, "Have you been here before?" Once they say yes or no, it's fine you say, "Ok great," then, go right into the mini presentation about the three or four points that practically everyone wants to know when they do business with you.

For example, someone walks through your door and you say, "Hi, have you been here before" and they say, "No, I haven't" and you say, "Ok, since you haven't been here before let me tell you about these four key things. We offer these kinds of options, we offer this kind of financing, we offer this kind of discount club and we offer this kind of delivery availability. How quickly did you need something, etc."

You want to go right into giving a mini presentation right up front. The final portion should be a seamless transition into the information gathering or the exploratory questions.

Once again, the greeting should go right into gathering information, where you try to discover the prospect's desires, needs and goals in order to match them with the products and services that you offer. You're trying to gauge the willingness of the prospect to make a purchase on this particular day. You're trying to find out the products and services the prospect may or may not know they want, or need, in order to get the desired result.

So, when you start to have people ask these questions in these scripts, you don't want it to be a used car salesman pitch, you want it to come across as genuine and authentic.

The goal is to give them a greeting and a mini presentation, but you're also using that greeting to go seamlessly into these exploratory questions.

Exploratory Questions

Exploratory questions are when you're asking certain things to find out about the goals, needs and desires of the prospects—or the past customers—who just walked through your door.

You're asking those questions so that your sales person, or you, can make a product or services recommendation. It's best to have three or four products or services to offer that have a generally wider appeal but are also profitable. If you have 500 or more products, you can't expect your staff, or you, to remember that many products, but you can have them remember product groupings for general products that may solve a host of problems etc., or may have more of a wide appeal. But the recommendation needs to exactly match, or closely match, the information provided by the prospect.

So if they come in and say that they want this color, this quantity, this fabric, this option for a service, or they need service for this specific tax problem, whatever the answers are, you want to make sure you recommend something—or your staff recommend something—that closely matches the information provided by the prospect or past customer.

This is where it's important to have staff members who are experts at your product and at your business. This is where it's also important that they are on the same page, that you have them trained and that they're very experienced with inventory levels as far as availability, options, price points, different packages, those kinds of things go.

Low Pressure Close

The next part that you want to have in all of your scripts is a low pressure close. This could be as simple as saying to the prospect, "Which one do you think will work better for you?" Assume the prospect wants the product, or service, but simply needs a little information. It's a different mindset, don't assume that they are just looking, but assume that they are coming into your business, that they are calling, that they are online and searching because they really need something from you.

This is a very non confrontational way of closing a sale by asking them which one. You could also ask them questions like, "Well, we could have someone come out and meet with you, or we could set an appointment for Thursday or Friday". You could ask those types of questions to make an assumptive close; that's non confrontational. While you're doing that, find out what other products or services the prospect may or may not know they want to reach their desired result as well.

Upsells, Down sells and Cross sells

Up sales are the services that can be added to customers purchases that will increase the average size of their order. For example, if they order a specific package, then you have an opportunity to say, "Listen, I know you ordered this package, but you're also going to need X, Y and Z to make that particular package work efficiently and effectively."

Down sells are when a product or service is offered to a customer who doesn't purchase the initial offer. Usually it's a lower price point, and a scaled down version of the up sale. So you may offer a whole kit caboodle, bells and whistles included type package, but then a customer says, "Hey, that's more than what I needed, it's a little bit more than I wanted to spend," or "that's a little bit too much for me".

You may want your sales people, or yourself, to have a script to say, "Ok, well in some cases, when that doesn't work for someone, they may go for option B." Option B can still be profitable while also being a good bargain for the customer, but it can also be a great deal for you as well.

Lastly, there are cross sales. Cross sales usually are a complimentary product or service that matches the initial purchase that the customer made.

It's like getting an alignment done with your car and you go on and get your tires changed at the same time; it just goes with car maintenance. Not crucial, but it will make your car run a little better; it's not imperative that you get done, but it just complements buying new tires.

Keep in mind that if you skip the step of documenting and organizing your sales presentations and closing systems actually turn these leads into profits, it was all for nothing. So don't cheat yourself, go through these processes and do what you need to do, but make sure that you're creating these scripts.

Phase two is taking inventory.

You need to make a list of your current staff in order to know what needs improving. You need answers to questions like:

- Which one of them would resist change the most?
- Would your staff enjoy a little challenge in terms of earning more income?
- Who gets the most positive feedback from customers and clients? And,
- Who generates business on their own.

These are all things you need to know before you get going. These are things that you need to know about your own staff members.

Many business owners don't want to track their success or failures because the truth hurts too much. Maybe it's a family member, maybe it's someone you really care about who has been around forever and they're just dragging you down but you don't want to track it because you know what it's going to show.

Real lasting change has to come from the leader and that's you. Be ready to handle things hands on when directing a new business. Remember, I told you when we started, this is about new attitudes new directions, new business focus.

Once you've created your training binder for your staff and your workers, schedule a meeting with your staff. This meeting doesn't have to be complex or complicated, just announce that you are going to make a few changes that are going to allow everyone to make more money.

Keep in mind that your employees come to work to make more money; they don't come just to hang out. They are there as an opportunity to make more money. By the way, if they are not there to make more money, then you need to take some time and really consider the future of that specific employee.

Prepare ahead of time for this meeting with one of your best employees in order to do some role playing.

Also be sure to let everyone know that you will be tracking the success or failure of everything. After all, you can't improve what you don't even measure and track.

By the way, you should be tracking the leads sales and profits of each advertisement campaign and sales presentation. You should be tracking them daily, weekly, monthly. You should know exactly what's generating what, what's working, what's not working. You need to know exactly the results that you're getting from the presentations that you're going to be tweaking. Let the staff know in this meeting that you're going to be tracking exactly what's going on with the leads, what happens when you ask questions and things like that to let them know that now it's a different era.

But here's the harsh reality; in order to improve your business and it grow profits, you may have to replace some employees. You may lose a few good employees who may not want to make the necessary changes needed for your business.

Also, you have to change the way you manage your business; you have to invest in regular and ongoing training for your employees. You have to protect your own success mindset by working with the business closely to help you navigate the minefield. It's a new reality; it's a new focus.

Chapter 8 - The Benefits of Email Marketing

So, why exactly should you use email marketing for your business? Email marketing holds all the benefits of the traditional marketing campaigns, but more! Below is a list of the main benefits you'll get from email marketing, but these are just the obvious ones. Once you start implementing your own campaign, you'll most likely find many, many more!

- **Low Cost.** Imagine how much you'd pay for a TV or radio commercial, or even a print ad. Email marketing costs next to nothing—even with the cost of your internet connection and email marketing guru taken into consideration!

- **Speedy.** With traditional marketing campaigns, you have to either wait to get your message out to the masses, or wait for those masses to randomly come across your ad. Email takes just seconds, everyone knows that. So when you send out an email campaign, your message is delivered in seconds.

- **Easy.** All business people have sent an email and know just how easy it is—that's why it's the preferred form of communication for just about everyone, not just business people! But email marketing is also very easy for the recipient of the email too. All they have to do is open it and read it. It doesn't interrupt their favorite program, it doesn't distract them while they're driving, and it doesn't annoy them when they're trying to listen to their favorite radio program. They see it and they choose to open it or not. *But,* if you've put the proper thought into your campaign, the chances are good that they will open it!

- **Personalized messages.** Unlike other forms of advertising, where you have to create a "blanket" message for all of your customers, you can tailor and personalize your email message to specific customers. This makes your customers feel like you've put in an extra effort to take their needs and concerns into consideration.

- **Viral.** Everything "goes viral" on the Internet and that includes email messages. Once you send the email to one customer, they could send it to another person and another and another and another.

- **Tracking.** Every part of an email marketing campaign can be tracked, including whether the email was opened, when it was opened, what links were clicked and if anything came from those clicks. Try tracking a radio ad—it's much more difficult, if not impossible.

Opt-ins. Email marketing campaigns often come with an opt-in, meaning that the customer may choose to be part of the campaign. When you start a campaign with the customer *wanting* to be a part of it, you're already well ahead of the game.

The Do's & Don'ts of Email Marketing

Along with everything already covered in this book, there are a number of small details that you should take care of to ensure that your email marketing campaign is as successful as you need it to be. We've broken these down into bite-size do's and don'ts.

Do:

- Ask what a customer's interests are at the time that they subscribe to your service. It will help you target your marketing campaign more successfully and help ensure that your customers actually read the email.

- Ask your customer what time is the best for them to receive email. Some may only check their email at work, leaving the weekend free for themselves, while others might prefer to leave it for the weekend because they're too busy at work.

- Ask customers how often they'd like to receive emails from you. Some want to be kept abreast of every news item and promotion you may have, while others may want to get only certain info in one concise email.

- Write for the customer, not your marketing campaign. Even though there's a certain product or service you're pushing, the email still needs to read as interesting and informative.

- Keep your subject line short and sweet, yet still hint at what they'll find inside the email.

- Include an area or a way for customers to leave feedback. It's always good to know what your customers are saying and thinking about you and it lets your customers know that you value their opinions.

- Keep the emails themselves short. A couple of paragraphs—between 5 and 10 sentences—is plenty of room to get your point across.

- Use a P.S. at the end of every email. Many customers will skim through the email quickly, but will pay close attention to the P.S. in order to get the gist of the message.

- Be personable! No one wants to read an advertisement that's landed in their inbox, but they will appreciate a friendly and sincere message from a friend.

- Use e-courses. These are a series of short emails that give one small piece of helpful information with every message.

- Email on Tuesdays and Wednesdays (for those customers who don't have a preference.) These days have been proven to have the best open rate.

Don't:

- Send irrelevant content. Your emails should always have a purpose and should never be sent expressly for the point of just sending email.

- Make misleading statements in your email. This will destroy the trust your customers have in you and will break the relationship forever.

- Use strategies to break spam filters. You shouldn't be sending spam (ever!) and so, you don't need to waste time figuring out how to trick the filters.

- Ever share your customer's information with anyone else. Again, this will permanently break the trust and the relationship you have with your customers.

Chapter 9 - Reputation Management

Have you taken time to see what consumers are saying about your company online?

If not, you could be losing sales and not even know it. Today, most consumers go online to see what others have to say before choosing a company to do business with.

In fact, over 70% of consumers trust online reviews as much as personal recommendations from people they know. Due to this fact alone, your company must do everything you can to ensure that you have a strong, solid, online image.

Are you investing in expensive, traditional advertising methods—such as Yellow Pages, Television, Radio, or Newspaper ads—and are not seeing any results?

The problem probably isn't with your ads; it could be what consumers are reading about you online. Advertising is just the first step that allows you to reach consumers; the next hurdle is gaining their trust so they will choose your company over your competition.

With online reputation management, you can increase local consumer attention to your business in ways you've probably never imagined.

Have you ever gone online to check out a local business, product or service? If so, did you read the reviews about the companies—or did you ignore them? If you're like most consumers, you read them. Not only that, but you probably trusted those reviews and used them to help you make a decision.

The same process flow happens when people are searching for YOUR type of business in the area. However, if you're not paying attention to what is being said, you have no way to soften the blow should something negative come up.

This is why online reputation management is no longer an option in today's internet savvy environment. In fact, it is a MUST if you want to operate at your full potential and consistently bring in new customers.

You're probably thinking, *Online reputation management is expensive and unnecessary for small businesses.* However, this is not true at all.

In fact, using online reputation management is extremely cost-effective compared to the expenses your business could acquire if your reputation is severely damaged. In addition, the sales you lose because of a negative online image could eventually cripple your ability to bring in profits.

By implementing some simple online reputation methods, you could take your business to another level.

Furthermore, online reputation management will help you establish credibility and trust amongst potential customers, as well as give your company a more memorable identity while building your brand.

Regardless of the type of products or services you offer, it would be a very costly mistake to ignore what is being said about you online. In fact, it could be outright *damaging.*

Can you imagine missing out on thousands of dollars in profits, just because you didn't take the time to monitor and manage your online image? Can you really miss out on such an opportunity?

Remember, if you're not making an effort to maintain a positive overall reputation, some of your competitors are. If a local consumer had to choose between a company with a negative image vs. one with an outstanding image, which one do you think they would choose? It's time for you grab your share of the local market and protect your online image today!

Make it Easy for Your Happy Customers to Leave Reviews

"Would definitely go here again. The food was AMAZING!"

"I HIGHLY recommend (insert your business name)!"

If you own a business, this is what you want to see showing up on review sites regarding your products and services. If you're suffering from a negative reputation online, the best thing you can do to counteract that negativity is to start getting more positive reviews like those above.

The problem is that it can be hard to entice your happy customers to post things about you online. This is usually because they're busy or just don't think it's important.

However, simply by asking, you can get more of your satisfied customers to go online and tell the world how they feel about your company.

Here are some tips to get you started on the path to more reviews:

The best thing you can do to get better reviews, is to help your customers along with the review process. For instance, you could give them some tips on actually submitting reviews for your company—such as which review sites to go to.

The easier you make it, the more likely it is that they will take the opportunity to give your company a review. Don't ask for too much information though, as this could be a turn-off.

In fact, make sure you mention the fact that this will be a "simple, easy process that should only take a few minutes of their time."

If there is any way you can collect customer reviews right at the point of sale, this is a powerful strategy as well. This way, your customers won't have to wait until they get home to write a review for you.

Social media is another way to simplify getting customer feedback. The internet is quickly becoming a more social place; more time is spent on Facebook and Twitter everyday than any other combination of websites on the internet. Facebook has over 1 billion users; this means that social media should be one of your highest marketing priorities.

If you have a poor reputation, whether through reviews, comments, or on social media, social networking can be an effective way to start getting more positive mentions.

Put social buttons all around your site and any other content you publish online—this makes it extremely easy for your customers to go to your social media profiles and say something nice. It also makes it easy for them to share your company with their social network connections.

To learn more and access resources click here
www.MyMarketingSystems.com

Chapter 10 - How to Make Customers Raving Fans with Referrals

Referrals are the second easiest customer to close. So why don't business owners spend more time creating systems to consistently produce referrals? Once again, the harsh reality—like most successful business building strategies—is that it takes real work and real changes, so many business owners avoid it like the plague. The closest most businesses get to referral business is the "friends and family" sale. But those fail because customers don't bring in anybody because there's no real benefit to doing so. Ninety-nine point nine percent of businesses don't have a single system in place to generate referral business. Most businesses are terrible at consistently generating referrals. These are the harsh facts and harsh reality.

When you're not generating referrals, you're really missing the boat. You're losing advantage and you're really losing out on easy advertising at little to no cost. It's less expensive to generate referrals from existing customers than to try to get new customers. Referrals close at a much higher rate because they've already decided to purchase from you based on the recommendation from their friend or family member. When you create a referral marketing system, you also create an awesome customer service environment that builds and strengthens existing customer loyalty.

Most business owners have no real commitment to getting referrals. They have too much focus on selfish reasons. To get referrals you have to focus on what your customers want, how you can reward them and the things that are important to them in order for them to refer you. A lot of business owners and sales staff don't even remember to ask for referrals and the business service or product is not something customers can honestly recommend to others because the quality is not there and the consistency is not there. The last thing is assuming that a great service or product alone is enough. It's not. You need more than that. You need a system in place. I know some business owners, as I talk to them, are afraid of asking for referrals. Those are some of the things that are making a lot of businesses unworthy of receiving referrals.

Here's the golden rule you should be striving for.

Level 1: Attracting suspects.

Level 2: Converting prospects.

Level 3: Taking care of first-time customers.

Level 4: Inspiring iron-clad loyalty.

Level 5: Creating customer referrals.

Those are the levels. Many of the strategies in this system talk about attracting suspects, or attracting prospects if you want to call it that. Then, with the sales staff and sales team and sales tools that you should be creating, you're going to convert prospects.

Level 3 is really providing what you say you can do—providing the service or providing the product that's reliable, and then inspiring iron-clad loyalty. Generating referrals should be the ultimate goal of all your marketing campaigns. Yes, it's fine to get the one sale today and to get the one sale tomorrow, but you want your customers to become raving fans and walking billboards for your company.

How to Build Your Referral Generating System

Step 1: Create a list of ideal referral candidates. It's a proven fact that some clients or customers will send referrals to your business while others won't. You have to narrow that down. Start by creating a list of profitable customers or clients who are most likely to refer you to others. If you have no way to narrow your list down, then start with a list of the past 12-24 months of your most recent customers or clients. That's a good starting place. Then, try to pinpoint people who have already sent you referrals. That way you have a basis or standard bar that you can match up other referral potential partners with.

Step 2: Create a compelling referral message. This could be your business USP but you may also choose to build your referral program around a big benefit. For example, if you own a limo service, your referral USP could be, "We will get you to your destination on time or it's free." So if one customer uses that service and was happy with it, they could turn to their friend and say, "Listen, the good news is if they don't get you there on time, it's free." So that's a USP that's easily transferrable, that is strong and compelling. Then, focus on what you can do for the customer, not what the referral means to you. So you want to make sure not only the customer will refer you but that you have systems, rewards and processes in place to get the customer who referred that customer to you a bonus, some type of benefit for doing so.

Step 3: Decide on how you will reward your referrals. In order to create a successful referral rewards system, you must know your customers or clients. Some people may get offended at being ethically bribed with gift cards, cash, discounts, etc. Avoid making the rewards program small and trivial. I know some rewards programs give out little trinkets and things. Most times those are not as effective as they could be because people don't put a high value on those things. Here's a good way to kind of gauge it. If you sell a luxury item or luxury service, then give classy rewards—bottle of wine, massage vouchers, etc. On the other hand, if you sell a commodity product or service, then you can give away lesser value rewards like a discount or inexpensive gift cards, or you could give away key chains—those kind of lower value things that people normally associate with the value that they're spending. So, if someone bought a Mercedes from you, then you wouldn't want to give them a five dollar Starbucks gift card. It's just not going to communicate the level of quality that they will get for sending you referrals.

A quick note on rewarding the people who refer customers or clients to your business: Let's look at LTV (lifetime value) again. If the lifetime value of our customer is something like $2500, then would you be willing to reward a customer or a referrer with a $50 cash voucher for referrals they sent you that actually purchased?

Think about it again.

If you made $2500 from every customer over the life of their time doing business with you, would you be willing to reward the person who referred them with a $50 cash voucher for referrals? Most business owners are too short time with their thinking to see the golden opportunity with their strategy. Most business owners would say no to that. But a savvy business owner and a smart business owner would say, "I would trade $50-$100 every day of the week for a $2500 customer."

When you crunch your numbers, it starts to be a big impact on your business. Five referrals who buy $2500 over their lifetime with you equals $12,500 in revenue. But you only paid out $250-$500 in cash vouchers to the referring customer. You could make it so that the referring customers in this case would have to spend a certain amount to redeem their voucher. So, if you don't feel comfortable with giving out cash vouchers to your business, gift cards, etc., you could make it so that the referring customer has to come back to your business and spend a certain amount to redeem their vouchers. I personally wouldn't recommend that, but sometimes you wouldn't want ten people redeeming their vouchers on the same day at your place of business. That many might make you short on cash, but the principle would still be the same.

You would still want to make sure that it's easily accessible— maybe it's a gift card, a Visa gift card, an American Express gift card for that $250 bonus. But you have to be thinking in a way of, is it a great trade?

So, the question is not would you trade $250-500 for $12,500? Hopefully that's a no brainer. But the real question is, how many times would you want to trade $250-500 for $12,000? Hopefully, the answer you're thinking of is, "As many times as I can and as fast as possible." This is part of that new mindset that you need to adopt to be successful in that new marketplace. Many business owners would not do it. They would not have a referral marketing program that pays any customer cash, for any number of reasons. But it's definitely a positive way to do it. It keeps people incentivized and motivated to keep referring.

Step 4: Create a system to create referrals into customers. The value is not in getting the referral by itself but in actually converting the referral into a customer or client. Start with one of your existing scripts of presentations and customize it for referral use. Be sure to include a mention of what the referral qualifies you for by being a referral. You should invest valuable training time, making sure your scripts or presentations are polished and professional.

A word of caution: referrals sometimes have a higher expectation of service. So it's best to have everyone on the same page in your office, or place of business, about actual delivery and the higher expectation of service for someone who comes referred.

Step 5: Develop your referral follow up system. You need to create several marketing pieces based on your core referral marketing message. Make it all about the benefit your customer gets from referring people to you and the benefit the referral will receive.

So once again, if you were the limo company and your USP was about getting your customers on time guaranteed or it's free, then you want to make sure that, when you're sending out your marketing pieces to your ideal customers for referrals, you mention that if they refer five people they may get a limo ride for free.

But, on the other hand, if you don't get their friend there on time, then their friend gets the limo ride for free. You want to make sure that your marketing pieces are all about the benefits your customer gets for referring people to you and the benefits the referral will receive.

Find a creative way to keep your core referral message in front of all your clients and customers, whether it's a newsletter, weekly e-mails, etc. You could use post cards, letters, emails or text messages, to follow up with your past clients to let them know all about your referral follow up system.

Your referral campaign should always be going out to your new customers. As soon as you get them in your system, you want them to get going on the system. For example, as soon as they buy from you, you want them to keep going and they should always be generating leads from these referral sources.

Conclusion

It is consistently being proven that, with the correct implementations of formulas and systems, any business can get more customers and get current customers to purchase more often. Many businesses are successfully growing their businesses with the proven formulas and systems.

Without going too far out on a limb, I think that it is safe to say that, "The successful and profitable businesses are willing to do what the unsuccessful businesses aren't willing to do, or, worse yet, don't even know about doing..."

A tested and proven method of becoming successful is modeling successful people. While subscribing to the "one-size-fits-all" doesn't apply, there are tested & proven formulas that consistently work effectively for most small businesses. When used correctly, the formulas allow small business owners to more accurately target their marketing efforts and to more accurately measure their advertising return on investment ROI. This type of accuracy is very effective and consistently profitable and it costs much less than traditional advertising and promotion methods.

Effective and profitable customer acquisition marketing strategies are successfully practiced by companies such as McDonald's, Apple, Starbucks, Nike and many others (including smart mom & pop sized businesses). Their formulas are all customer focused. Their formulas also help business owners identify their best Unique Selling Propositions USP. Knowing your business's unique selling propositions gives you the "meat" of your marketing messages. For example, McDonald's told us "You deserve a break today" and "We love to see you smile." They sell hamburgers—but, they have clearly identified their USPs and use them to fuel their marketing messages to us.

Smart small business owners, equipped with the knowledge of the formulas and how to use them to set up customer acquisition systems, are not held hostage to the roller coaster effect of feast or famine that so many unequipped small business owners are. When your systems are in place, your business will see dramatic customer purchasing—both from getting new customers and current customers purchasing more often.

Formulas produce business specific customer acquisition systems; practiced customer acquisition systems consistently produce growing profits.

In my opinion, the impediment that prevents you, as a small business owner, from being able to take a clear and honest look at your business is the exact element that has taken your business this far—your unwavering love for and commitment to your business. Like loving, protective parents, you "know" your business better than anyone else does. You "know" the good and the bad. You are convinced that "no one else knows your "baby" as well as you do." That is a normal "protective factor" for you.

However, that "protective factor" does not allow us to correctly use the formulas that ask us questions that are better answered by our customers. As a rule, small business owners feel we "know" the best answers about our business. For example, customers will provide much more accurate answers to being asked why they do business with you than you, as business owner (and protector) would answer. Formulas help us to survey our customers for the actual correct answers about why they do business with you. With those correct answers, you can then create your marketing messages, targeting your perfect customer types.

The correct use of the formulas will then help you to set up systems specific to your business, to your USP and to your targeted marketing strategies. This is the formula and systems approach practiced by the consistently growing businesses—and now, it is available to smart business owners like you.

The Beginning!

Get your unannounced bonuses and find out more about the "Small Business Marketing TOUGH LOVE SYSTEM: The Ultimate Business Growth Training System For Small Business Owners" click here www.MyMarketingSystems.com

Get 20 FREE Small Marketing Videos at www.BusinessGrowthMarketingStrategies.com